TRAUMAS OF A
FATHERLESS
CHILD

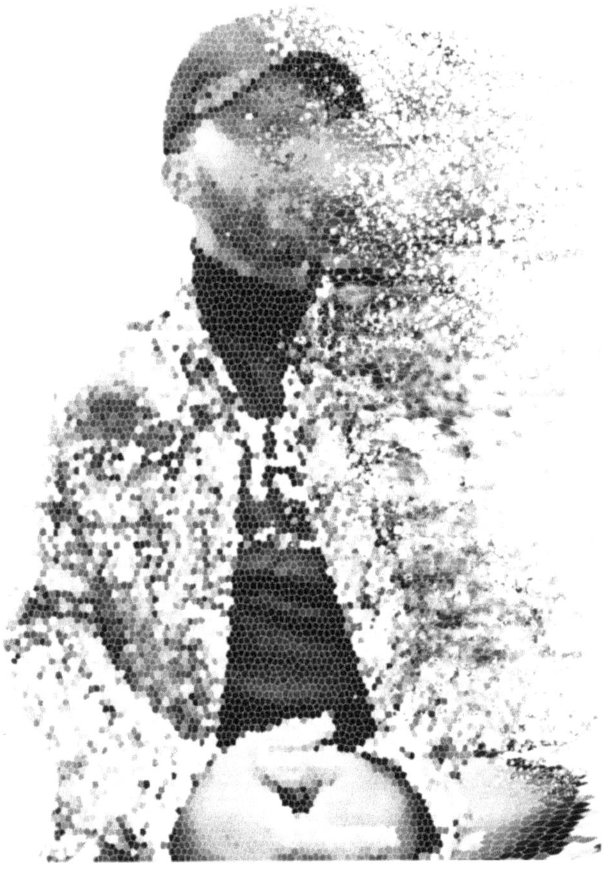

Traumas of a Fatherless Child

poetry collection by
JUSTIN SCOTT

Copyright © 2020 by Justin Scott
Published/Formatting by BlackGold Publishing

All rights reserved. No part of this book may be
reproduced, scanned,
or distributed in any printed or electronic form without
permission.
First Edition: February 2020
Printed in the United States of America
ISBN: 978-1-7345083-2-1

table of contents

dedication
vii

I 2
The Elegance of A 3
Do You See Me? 4
Confessions To God 5
Rewritten 6
Life Lessons 7
Strength 8
Our First Kiss 9
Her Peace 10
Her Quiet Place 11
Rooftop 12
Healing 13
Letting It Out 14
Safe Haven 15
Love Cautiously 16
Black Boy 17
The Mistake 19
Someone Like You 20
I Love You 21
Walk This Earth for You 22
II 23
Scars 24
Titanic 25
My Piece Within 26
A Mother's Scorn 27
Scars Pt II 28
Finding Herself 29
Floating On Dreams 30
The Truth Within Love 31
Reincarnate 32

God's Regret 33
Unknowing 34
A Poem to My Father.. 35
Pride 36
Black Girl 37
The Truth 38
Rewind 39
Can You Stand the Rain? 40
The Morning After 41
The Greatest Advice 42
III 43
I Promise 44
Dear Black Women 45
A Late Night Write.. 46
Conversations at The Dinner Table 47
Why Don't Your Relationships Last? 48
I Trust You 49
Unjustified Crimes 50
Why Did You Hurt Me? 51
Why I Stare at You Without Speaking 52
Blackbird (A Dedication Poem) 53
Your Smile... 55
I Need You 56
Why Didn't You Stay Over? 57
What I've Noticed 58
Stranger 60
Where It All Ends... 61

acknowledgment
63

dedication

For Morgan,

I hope that I've became the man
you've prayed that I'll be.

Traumas of a Fatherless Child

I

The Elegance of A

Black Boy

Whom plants Lilacs in his mother's garden

Joyful Boy

That had the color of loyalty

Embedded into his skin.

Mama raised him right

To live with so much zest

But yet his eyes still fear

His destiny being rewritten

By that cold iron from the gun

That was meant to serve and protect him.

Do You See Me?

There is no beauty in the eyes of the beholder
Because I saw myself in my father's casket.

I wonder if the woman I fell for

Saw the pureness in my heart,

Thru the cracks I made in hers…

I wonder if God saw me at all.

Confessions To God

I've prayed to him
Palms together
With broken glass lodged in them
From every heart I've intentionally shattered
Praying that I feel the pain I caused.

Rewritten

It's not the fact that the story has ended,

But you dared to change the author

As if he was allowed to let his peen bleed thru
This cover we've created.

Please if you may

Place this book on the shelf

Even if it collects dust

At least you'll be able to

Go back and relive the memories

That we shared.

Life Lessons

My mother taught me at a young age

I am no nigger,

But a man.

She is my lighthouse in my darkest hours.

Her voice

Powerful

Yet the pain in her silence

Cuts like a machete thru the heart.

Over the years she learned to let go

She refreshed her life

Like an apricot on a warm summer day.

I thank you for building me into the man I am
Brick by brick.

I pray my mind becomes as strong as yours.
The day you take flight to the Heavens

I know God will rejoice.

Strength

A soft-spoken woman

With a smile that resembles

Pink tulips blossoming during Springtime

Heartbroken from being fatherless

But strong enough to teach me how

To love my father more.

A mind of a true queen

With a treasure between her pelvis

Made from my ribs

You were born to heal

And to be loved unconditionally.

Our First Kiss

She asked

"Do I remember our first kiss?"

I told her...

Her lips were like Azaleas

Pink

Fragile...

So I kissed you with caution

No need to forget that

Paris in Springtime

Still holds magic

And I'm not the one to take

My heart on a trip

It isn't prepared for.

Her Peace

If you can't love her thru her storm
Don't disturb her when she's at peace.

Her Quiet Place

Her demons were the biggest battles she ever faced
Even her shadows faded from her

Far earlier than the sunset did.

The only place she felt safe was

In a room that painted the color quiet.

Where her walls kept secrets from

every lover that took a piece of her soul.

Rooftop

She was lost in her thoughts

Sitting on a rooftop bar

Where the breeze

Kissed her skin

Better than the man

That keeps buying her broken promises.

Healing

Many days I've felt as if I was superman

But I've learned that I am more man than hero

With a mind that has captured many broken hearts
But not have the strength to heal any of them

… Not even my own.

Letting It Out

I'm sorry if you don't understand

But things have been boiling in my chest

For many moons

And I finally have the courage to let it out...

I never knew how to love

No, there was no song in this young boy's voice.
It took half my life to understand prayer

And even then I prayed to end my life

More than I prayed to live it.

Safe Haven

I had to remind myself

There is a light inside of you

Don't allow it to wither away

Let your words become a sanction

A place where even God doesn't

fear to send his Angels to.

Love Cautiously

I've learned over the years

That you have to tip-toe thru love.

That even in a crowded room

It can be a ticking time bomb

And I don't know how much time
I have left with you.
Even the sunset we watch together
will eventually…

Furl onto you and me.

And that too will die

But for now…

Love me until eternity escapes through our bones

Then and only then

Will our love grow

As a rose does within concrete.

Black Boy

You will not die here black boy

400 years of being broken and battered

Yet, we still walk in our ancestor shoes

As if we had Jim Crow in our palms...

I know your soil is tired...

I know America treats us as if

We have gunshot as a skin color.

And a residue from an officer

That has "the biggest fear of

Being next to an unarmed black boy"

Left on our bodies.

He goes home, preparing for Sunday morning

Where he sits at the head of the table
praying for his protection.

As that same black boy's grandmother,

Prepares for Sunday mourning

As she prays to God for answers.

Understand

Black Boy

Our privileges are different

It lies on the brink of Birmingham in the 60's

Speak Up!

But we plead and implore thee

Don't Shoot!

We Ride!

Until we gain the skill of not falling again.

Remember,

A great man wrote a letter in a four-cornered cell

That paved the way for our freedom...

Don't let them corner you into a cell

Black Boy

Don't let them tell you that you're nothing

You are a king

Negus from the Original Land

Even if a thousand stars go Supernova

You will rise from the heat of those flames

You will rise...

You will rise...

Phoenix in the skies

You will rise

And

Show the true meaning of

Black Boy.

The Mistake

I wonder do you look at yourself in the mirror
And ask yourself if you're a good guy?

Did you see her heart as a temple

Or

A place where you could cover your sins

And pretend to be a God for her?

Were you trying to heal her

Or

Were you trying to find someone to comfort your demons?

She wasn't here to save you...

She was there to help you find your light

That you always hidden

But once you found it

You left her in the darkness

To find herself again

After she lost herself in you.

Someone Like You

I've prayed for someone like you

Way before Adele found her voice
Within her ex-lover hands

Like back when our ancestors looked to the
Northern Star for guidance

The same star that led me to you.

I love you

Falls on the lips of a believer

That kisses their spouse as if

Eternity was right around the corner

It's like understanding how God works

It may be complicated at first

But it's a lifetime of joy
Once you hear it from someone

That means it wholeheartedly.

Walk This Earth for You

Even without breath

I will walk this earth for you

Even if the moon and the night sky
Becomes black

And there was no Northern Star

To guide me to you…

I will use the prayers from our ancestors

As if we were destined to be together
Centuries ago.

II

Scars

Her lips blessed too many men

That have cursed her purity

Men...

Whom covered their hidden intentions

Behind a smile

Which led her to give them her all

And with each man

They left her with pain

That pierced thru her soul.

Since then,

She hasn't recognized herself

From too many broken mirrors and promises.

In the end

She will use her heart less

Before any man makes her heartless

But, can you blame her

For having scars nobody can heal?

Titanic

Your beauty is unique

Like a rose growing in a royal garden

I know people have tried to control your life

Not knowing that your mind is like
A night before a revolution.

It holds the peace between self and reality.

This world doesn't see your smile

That shines just as bright

As the diamond that falls

Right above your chest.

I know your biggest fear

Is being played like a game of Poker

But there is hope in this gamble

An unforeseen love story Of an artist that found life

In the depths of your eyes

A love that wasn't destined to crash

But it did...

We knew we were sinking

And there was no ship

That could keep us afloat

But I promise unto eternity I will never let you Go.

My Piece Within

I can't get high enough

To settle my sins anymore

This piece

Is my only peace of mind

Stuck between

Wanting to know more

And needing to know less

About who I am.

Nevertheless

I'm still seeking God in the darkness

While the darkness seeks me.

I only pray that this peace

Finds its way to the light.

A Mother's Scorn

She watched her mother's eyes

Fill up with tears of pain

And watched how her mother

Broke down her smile

While giving up her heart to a man

...A man

That stood over her as if she were ashes

Under a dying flame.

Since then,

She grew up to talk, walk, and

Look like her mother

With the same broken smile

That made you believe

She carried her mother's mistakes.

Scars Pt II

She learned to cover her scars

From every man

That ripped away at her dignity

She hid her hands during prayers

Hoping that no one saw

The dirt underneath her fingernails From

crawling back to each man

That left her in the darkness.

That made her feel less than who she was.

Finding Herself

What is God to her?

A man that has no intention of
Loving her correctly

That only pleases her when he
Is between her thighs.

With a sinners tongue
She calls out his name

She scratches her mistakes into his back
Hoping that he has the bone to fix them.

When it's done

She praises the moonlight
But curses the morning sun

Because she wakes up to a half-empty bed

With less of a will to care

If another man fills the void the last lover left.

But what's left is nothing...

She sits and wishes

A man will come in and truly cum in

Her life for the better.

Allowing her to confide in him

With the secrets that her past holds so close to
Her Heart.

Floating On Dreams

Some nights I wonder
Do butterflies have dreams?
How can a starfish lose its head
And still resurrect as himself?
Because I've lost my mind too many times
Not knowing who I was.
Yet,
I dreamt of these beautiful scenes
Where you and I connected
Like two perfect rainstorms.

The Truth Within Love

She walked to me like a sunrise

And the only thing I could do

Was embrace the warmth in her smile

While I stared into her eyes

Glistened with tears from a wasted love

She knew I could feel her pain

Because I held on to her like

A cold wind wrapping around

Two lovers

That didn't want to let each other go.

But they knew the end was near

So she sunk into my chest

Tears bleeding thru my shirt

My lips pressed gently on the crown

Of her forehead

Reminding her

That a gentle love

Walks with patience

So she held me tighter

Knowing the truth

That I couldn't love her in any way

Because what was love anyway?

Reincarnate

I wish I could die in your eyes

Resurrect as a flower

Hope that you see and pluck me from the enriched soil

Place me on your favorite love poem

So I can see why

Your heart pumps marathons of blissful words.

God's Regret

I've made love to you
With her on my mind
I know God whispers to himself
Why do I continue
To bless this man with an
Angel I took time to create?

Unknowing

My mother never questioned why
I hugged her so tightly
She never knew how close she was
From hugging me for the last time.

A Poem to My Father

If I could write a letter to my father
I'll let him know how far I've come
How far I have to go
That his shoes are the biggest ones
I never want to fill.

Pride

I created this burning desire to hate you
But one day I know I'll have to forgive you.

Black Girl

Black Girl Magic
Skin the color of royalty
Superior to the touch
But they tried to convince you
That your type of beauty doesn't belong here.

The Truth

Too many nights I've woke up

With death beside me.

I don't know if it's from

The liquor that I've found in my mother's room

The same liquor that drowned out the pain
From the beatings she endured

Or

The fact that I feel like I'm slowing fading away.
The truth is...

I've ended my life so many times in peace
Within the darkness

And no one was here to stop me.

I cried out my father's name

As if his angel wasn't already there with me.

I turned myself into
The black sheep of my family

Because they wouldn't understand me anyway.

Rewind

There is a stillness in the air

No heartbeat in this body of mine.

This pain resonates far deeper than any knife
Cutting thru the heart

This is how I felt when you left me

Your last goodbye became the closest

Thing I feared

Beside hearing God's voice for the first time.

If this is it,

Then tell me you love me

So I can rewind the hands of time

To when it all started

Hoping that we can feel real love one last time.

Can You Stand the Rain?

She smiled when I asked her

"Can you stand the rain?"

Because she knew

Just like the flowers

With enough love and attention

She will bloom just as beautiful.

And I was willing to give her what she deserved.

The Morning After

The morning came like a silent storm

After the night we made love for hours

You woke up next to me

Not knowing if you made a mistake

Or

If you believed it was fate

But you took a chance to fall in love with me.

The Greatest Advice

I talked to my dad about you

He asked God for permission

To give me the greatest advice I've ever heard

He said

"The woman that you decide to give your life to love her like I could never love your mother.

I know you are not my mistakes

But you still hold a part of me.

So forgive me

And hold on to her

Like I held your mother's smile

until I took my last breath.

Never let her go

And if you fall to your knees

It only better be to thank God

Or

You better be asking the rights

To her ring finger."

I Promise

To always admire your beauty

Like the night sky admires the stars

To treat you as the Goddess you are

To love you as loudly as I can

And cherish our time we have together.

I promise

To worship the rain

That trickles down your skin

That lands on the ground you walk on.

I promise one day

I'll end up breaking this promise.

Dear Black Women

Have broken mirrors become all you see?

What pieces of you are not complete?

From every man that came into your life

And destroyed everything you built.

Since birth,

You were held by trembling hands

That never knew the pain your beauty hides.

We as men

Forgot the blessing of your presence

And treat you as if God didn't make you

For a reason

A reason beyond our mind

Truth is

All you want is love and protection

But we were taught to destroy

everything we come in contact with.

Even when the color of your skin

Is your heaviest burden most time

In the end

All you want is to confide in us

And all we do is come around to disappear.

Maybe one day it will change

When we realize that we can't live without you.

A Late Night Write

Some say it's a gift

I just say I have a passion in my fingertips,

That grasped at every inch of your heart.

Have you ever wondered why you fell for my words?
Darling'

Have you ever held a star
Or
Even sat upon the moon?
If not,

Fall in love with a poet Desire my every word
Free your heart

As my words fill the emptiness of your body
I'll surrender myself to you

I give you every poem every thought

That describes how perfect you are
So you will know I will never let a

Ocean
Storm

Nor sunrise or sunset
Stop me from bringing joy to your smile

Queen

Hold me close,
Like a New York's winter around us
And promise me
You'll never let go.

Conversations at The Dinner Table

My mother doesn't like talking about her
Abuse,

But you can hear it in the cracks of her voice
During prayers.

Why Don't Your Relationships Last?

Because it took me 20 years to understand
What faithfulness is.

And I still get nervous about the word
Commitment.

I Trust You

Because I put everything in your hands

Except for my father's voice

A forgotten treasure

A Lost jewel

But you taught me to never curse that man,
Because he created me

And without his absence

I would have never found my way to you.

Unjustified Crimes

38% of inner-city teens die every year

Lifeless bodies drop to the unbroken ground.
Their blood-soaked up in the same place

Where they found joy during the summertime.

Their screams haunt the silent sidewalks

And no rain can wash away the names.

Remember their names

Say them loud

Until their angels return.

Why Did You Hurt Me?

Because I hated myself so much

I didn't have the strength to love you.

Why I Stare at You Without Speaking

I'm imagining myself

Sitting on a blank canvas

Trying to create a beautiful masterpiece

Not a Mona Lisa or even a Ginevra de' Benci
But I'm creating you.

Blackbird (A Dedication Poem)

Say farewell, as the Blackbird sings.

Hold its voice, like a diamond

Because,

Death comes like a silent sunrise

And some people were taught to rejoice it and others to mourn it.

Because it's another day without the one you loved

Did you know,

That you left our souls empty

With tears of unanswered question run down our face?

Every breath we take without you hear

Feels like a mountain crushing our chest.

My heart is heavy as I write this poem,

Do you remember the time we talked for hours,

How we found peace on the corner of 30th and 15th?

When everything in my life was slowly burning down
You told me "God has us and we will make it."

But jokes on me

Because God has you

And all I'm left with is

Dreams that I could of cut the ropes of

depression from your neck

Before it took the innocence out of your smile.

That smile we have to recreate thru

Every brother and sister you left behind.

You left your twin with an empty reflection

Of who you were

Does he dare look into the mirror?

…Maybe one day he'll see you

With every reason

To still love you despite your selfish ways

But with every reason to believe that

God is real and makes no mistakes.

But this one time he did

He took a King from this earth

Without knowing he had a crown all long.

As the sunset

Over your casket

We shall sing

As the Blackbird says farewell.

Your Smile

Reminds me of everything beautiful I've ever known
That crescent shape moon stained on your face

I know you come alive in the night time.

I wonder if this is how Adam felt

When he first saw eve.

How safe he felt in her smile

No forbidden fruit

No tragic endings

Just a smile that I'm willing to get lost into.

I Need You

During my 3 a.m. thoughts

When I want you beside me

So I can caress the arches of your mind

And

Explore the inner curves of your thoughts.

While you hold me tighter

As I go deeper

Inside your secrets

I want you to scream your insecurities

Into my ear

So I know just how to love you right.

Why Didn't You Stay Over?

Because I knew by the morning

I would've forgot

Every lie I told you

To get you to love me.

Then, I'll be forced to tell the truth.

Stranger

Ever since I turned six

You've become a ghostly figment of my
Imagination

Somehow you created time portals

Where I could only hear your voice for

Moments

It broke my heart to hear that type of pain.

I hated how smoothly "I Love You Son" rolled
off your tongue

Words that I spent half my life trying to find the
meaning of.

Why'd you leave me in this world alone?

For me to fend for myself

Your unprotected seed in such a harmful
world.

I'm turning into you more and more each day
And I hate it just as much as my mother does.

What I've Noticed

I saw a woman

With beauty that can rip open galaxies

A smile so bright she made the stars insecure

Moonlight eyes

I could write to shapes of your pupils

Or

Maybe my words can orbit around your soul Like planets around the sun.

See every woman has a story

But this so happens to be for you.

With your sweet country accent

And the intelligence of a Harvard alumni

Ironic

Southerners aren't portrayed as being smart.

However, you are one in a million

Like the chances of being struck by lightning twice

You are rare

A diamond

That has been broken but yet still shines.

How dare someone say you're not royalty Queen

You take over kingdoms with the motion of your fingertips

You are in control.

Like the way your body moves

Gently

Yet elegant.

You create sexual fantasies in a young man's eyes

But please don't let that discourage you

Your body is a temple

That he Egyptians get jealous of

Thinking why couldn't we build something so glorious

But unfortunately you weren't built

You were slowly crafted by our highest

Because beauty takes time.

So when I finally see you

I'll get the courage to say

I want to die inside your smile

And resurrect in the joy that your laugh brings.

Tell me have you ever made love to a poet? Have you ever came 1,000 times in one night?

I want to make love to you

Like the sky is falling

And the angels applaud in unison

Saying this is how it's meant to be.

Where It All Ends

If I ever break down and give up
Remember my life was written in this poem.

This would be the truth...

In 2008 I lost my faith in God
When he took my father away
He took my faith with him.

For years I've been chasing
A voice I'll never be able to hear again.

This... This caused the start of
All the sinful acts I've made in my life.

I tried finding myself in the darkness
Without any light to guide me.

This is my story
My pain
Wrapped in a burning notebook.

This is why I've become distant from my family I've lost more love
in a place where
Love is supposed to always be.

If home is where the heart is
Then my heart stopped beating a long time ago.

It gets deeper from here.

I've coped with losing myself by trying to recreate The feeling of
being wanted in women
Who would of went to the end of the world for me.

But in my selfish ways I've broken their hearts
Destroyed what they believed what love was

And started writing poems about how much love we shared.
knowing my heart was never in my words.

I ask myself,
Is this why you can't sleep at night?

Does your past creep back up
Like a thief in the night?

I had to make them believe I was okay
Knowing I was dying inside.

I allowed myself to drown knowing that there Were so many people willing to save you...

It gets deeper,
My cousin killed himself a couple years ago
And a part of me feels like I should have left with him.

A selfish act
But the best way I wanted to escape my mind
My sins. My life.

But I found a reason to live

Because I have a story
That will change lives one day
A story filled with love.
So here I am,

Still searching for God

And some days I feel like I'm not too far away. Just know that

This is my fight This is my war

And I'm not scared anymore.

acknowledgement

I want to thank everyone that has motivated and supported me throughout this journey of mine. This section is dedicated to you and from the bottom of my heart I appreciate you all.

Thank you to my mother and sister. Carolyn and Jasmin Dias. For always having my back and giving me a reason to continue to live, love, and inspire others around me. I couldn't have finished this book without you both.

I also want to thank my support system who are near and dear to my heart. My dear friends, Joseph Cunningham Jr, Kevin Mobley, Rischard Brown, Sabrina Hilton, Dylan and Savannah Paquette, Sterling Cameron, and Dontrell Burgess.

Once again, I thank each and every one of you who has watched my progression and put in their input to making this book a success.

I love you all

—

Justin Scott is a lover, poet, friend and son. Throughout the years he has developed his voice through prose and delivers an impactful introduction through "Traumas of a Fatherless Child." Be sure to follow more of his by visiting us at blackgoldpublishing.com.